BAPTIZED:

MARKED FOR LIVING!

A Lent-Easter Reflection on Faith and Life.

by
Pastor John D. Hopper

Sacred Heart, Minnesota
1996

Baptized: Marked for Living!

FIRST EDITION
Copyright @ 1996 by
John D. Hopper

Scripture quotations are from the New Revised Standard Version of the Bible, copyright 1989 by the Division of Christian Education of the National Council of the Churches of Christ in the USA. Used by permission.

Library of Congress Catalog Card Number: 96-94314

ISBN 0-7880-0684-3   PRINTED IN U.S.A

Dedicated to Sally, Michael, Jennifer, and Sarah. Thank you for your love and support in our walk of faith as baptized children of God.

TABLE OF CONTENTS

ACKNOWLEDGEMENTS

My life as a child of God began when God washed me in the waters of baptism. The shape of the ordained ministry to which I have been called has been molded by a strong baptismal theology. The action of a gracious God has sustained me and guided me through over twenty years of service as a pastor in the former American Lutheran Church and now the Evangelical Lutheran Church in America.

The opportunity to preach God's Good News is a high privilege for which I am grateful. The opportunity of preaching a series on baptism during Lent on two occasions has been a rewarding experience for me and for those who participated in that worship experience with me.

The first occasion was in 1987 at Trinity Lutheran Church in Westbrook, MN. The series grew out of my Doctor of Ministry studies at Luther Northwestern Theological Seminary and was well received by the members of that congregation. They were extremely supportive of the work I was doing in baptismal theology and its practice there.

The second occasion for a Lenten-Easter series on baptism was at the Our Savior's-Opdal Lutheran Parish in Sacred Heart, MN., during the Lenten season of 1993. This time the members of the parish were invited to *"create"* a home altar with the baptismal items given to them after each worship service.

I am deeply grateful to Geneva Steinbach, an A.I.M. of our church, and secretary of the parish. She helped develop the symbols and organized the members of the parish into work groups to make the various items that were to be given to the families of the parish during the Lenten series. Her able help made the series possible.

I am also grateful to the members of the Our Savior's-Opdal Parish who responded so favorably to this opportunity to grow in baptismal faith and service. Their encouragement made the work of preparation and preaching a joy. It was an exciting Lenten season for all of us! May your journey through Lent be as rewarding as ours was in 1993.

Since that Lenten season a number of clergy have asked about this series. I have shared the idea with them. They have developed it for use in their particular settings. Though this material is usuable for a series during the Lent/Easter seasons, I also see it as useful as a weekly family devotional series focused on baptism. Families can make their own family "altar" and use these meditations for "family time" reflections on their lives as baptized servants of Christ.

Finally, thanks to my family for their loving support in my work as a pastor of the Church. They have encouraged me in the preparation of this manuscript for distribution in the larger church.

Shalom!

Pastor John D. Hopper
Sacred Heart, Minnesota
Easter Sunday 1996

INTRODUCTION

One of the most important pieces that Martin Luther wrote, and maybe one of his best writings, is <u>The Large Catechism</u>. Unfortunately far too few Lutheran Christians have read it. Of particular interest to me is a paragraph in the section on baptism. There Luther writes these words:

> *"In baptism, therefore, every Christian has enough to study and to practice all his life. He always has enough to do to believe firmly what baptism promises and brings- victory over death and the devil, forgiveness of sin, God's grace, the entire Christ, and the Holy Spirit with His gifts."* [1]

For Lutherans all of ministry, all of Christian living, has its foundation in God's action in baptism. All that God's people **ARE**, and can **BECOME**, and **DO**, grows out of God's gracious act of love in baptism. The drowning and the rising (the death of the old self and the resurrection of the new person) in baptism is the daily pattern of Christian existence.[2] Baptism ". . . now saves us . . ."[3] and calls us Christians into a "baptismal existence" that focuses daily life in service.

So, as Luther puts it, Christians have ". . . enough to study and to practice . . . enough to do to believe . . ." all that God has already done for all of us in baptism. It will take a lifetime of living to fulfill this baptismal covenant. The discipleship created by God in baptism is a cradle-to-grave existence. Just as John anointed Jesus for his ministry when Jesus was baptized in the Jordan River, so God saves and also anoints us for our daily ministry of love and service in the splashing of the water, the speaking of the Word, and the empowering of the Holy Spirit as we are baptized in the waters of the baptismal fonts in our churches. Luther explains the "miracle" of this washing with these words:

*"You shall take it (baptism) as a very special grace
that he should deal so kindly with you, so kindly that
none could ever be more kindly. For he simply
presents a person (man); he does not put a sword, a
gun, or any kind of weapon in his hand, but simply
commands him to take a little water with his bare,
empty hand and say these words, 'I baptize you in
the name of the Father, and of the Son, and of the
Holy Spirit. Amen.'"*[4]

Baptized into this "priesthood" ministry we are anointed for the
lifelong work of God's people in the name of Christ. As the
Lutheran service for "Holy Baptism" reminds us in its opening
words:

*"In Holy Baptism our gracious heavenly Father
liberates us from sin and death by joining us to the
death and resurrection of our Lord Jesus Christ. We
are born children of a fallen humanity; in the waters
of baptism we are reborn children of God and
inheritors of eternal life. By water and the Holy Spirit
we are made members of the Church which is the
body of Christ. As we live with him and with his
people, we grow in faith, love, and obedience to the
will of God."*[5]

So, what does it mean to **LIVE** as a Christian in our world
today? What shape of ministry truly reflects the Word of God as
the **LIVING WORD** in Jesus Christ? In other words, how can we
who have been named and claimed by God through baptism **be
and become** better stewards of the gifts and the life that the Lord
has given to us? Does the Lutheran tradition offer anything unique
to an understanding of what it means to be and become bearers of
the Word?

Luke, in the tenth chapter, tells a story of a lawyer who confronts
Jesus. This encounter gives us an excellent example of what it
means to be a member of God's family. As this conversation

develops Jesus is able to instruct all of us about the importance of loving service to our "neighbor".

The lawyer's initial interest is to trap Jesus with the Torah. The confrontation begins with a simple question: *"Teacher, what must I do to inherit eternal life?"* Of course, Jesus, as is his usual method, responds to the question by asking another question: *"What is written in the law? What do **you** read there?"* (my emphasis, and possibly also Jesus'?)

The lawyer responds, *"You shall love the Lord your God with all your heart, and with all your soul, and with all your strength, and with all your mind; and your neighbor as yourself."*

Ah, yes, that is correct. *". . .do this, and you will live,"* says Jesus.

For the lawyer that is more easily said than done. As with most human beings, the more important question becomes, "What's in it for me?" So, the discussion continues, "But wanting to *justify* himself, he asked Jesus, *'And who is my neighbor?'*"[6]

Translating the truth of the Word of God into living faith is often difficult. After all, what does faith have to do with how Christians live? What difference does faith in Jesus Christ make in daily living? Does simply knowing what the Word teaches translate into action? The lawyer knew the Torah. He knew what the Word of God taught. Did it lead him to live it? Was he able to transfer God's Word into action? Could he love his neighbor? Or, would he continue to make excuses for not loving his neighbor while dodging the real issue with inane questions like, "And who is my neighbor?" This question is inane because the Torah is clear about "who" the neighbor is,[7] and the lawyer knew the Torah. This question is a dodge because the lawyer seemed unwilling to make a change in his lifestyle even after this encounter with the living Word, Jesus.

This little incident between Jesus and the young lawyer is instructive for the present-day people of God as well. How is it that Christians can translate professions of faith in Jesus Christ (the heart of which is captured in the "Great Commandment" on the lips of the lawyer) into everyday actions? Professing to love God and neighbor, how do God's people do it? What is the relationship between salvation and stewardship? In other words, how can the Church be the Church? What is the basis of daily ministry? Where do God's people begin?

Jesus' story of the Samaritan, and his acts of love and kindness in helping the beaten, robbed, and half-dead Israelite who lay alongside the road between Jerusalem and Jericho, paints a picture of the basic form of baptismal discipleship. That basic shape is servanthood on behalf of others: **ALL** others, no matter who or where they are in the world; it includes even hated enemies. "Our redemption is precisely critical because it frees us to be a part of God's creative and sanctifying activity in the world, both in its private and public dimensions."[8]

This Lent-Easter preaching series, "Baptized: Marked for Living!", is an attempt to use the Lenten season as a time for reflection upon **WHO** we are as God's covenant children in baptism and **HOW** we are to live as people forever marked with the cross of Christ. The early Christian church used the Lenten season as a time of preparation for candidates to be baptized on Easter.[9] This Lent-Easter series may lead to a reaffirmation of baptism by members of the congregation on Easter Sunday.

The materials in this book are both theological and practical. The theological materials appear in the form of meditations for mid-week worship services beginning on Ash Wednesday and culminating with Easter Sunday. These worship services could be as a gathered congregation or as a gathered family in the home. The practical materials appear in the form of instructions for making a "home altar" using symbols that "carry" the theological "freight". The centerpiece is the cross to which another symbol is added each week. The "texts" for both the theological and practical aspects of the theme are from the service for "Holy Baptism" in the LBW and various biblical "baptismal" references.

In a world filled with pain and suffering, sorrow and hurt, God calls us, the baptized people of God, to bring the message of good news, of hope, of mercy, of God's grace into the lives of those around us. This is our calling. This is our work. This is our ministry as baptized persons- persons marked for living.

ASH WEDNESDAY

Baptized: Marked for Living!

SIGNED.

THE SYMBOL OF THE CROSS

What more appropriate symbol with which to begin our Lenten journey than the cross? We know that Jesus was crucified. He was hung on a cross to die. The cross has become the defining mark of the Christian faith. Paul talks about Christians having but one message, *". . .to know nothing among you except Jesus Christ and him crucified."*[10]

It is also true that the cross is used in a very specific way as part of the worship of Ash Wednesday in the church. The imposition of ashes, a reminder of our penitence and mortality[11], is often done in the shape of the cross upon each worshiper's brow. Thus, as we begin this Lenten season on Ash Wednesday, we reflect upon the symbol of the cross by which we have all been *SIGNED* in Holy Baptism.

THE MEDITATION

Paul writes to the Corinthian church:

> *"For the message about the cross is foolishness to those who are perishing, but to us who are being saved it is the power of God. For it is written, 'I will destroy the wisdom of the wise, and the discernment of the discerning I will thwart.' Where is the one who is wise? Where is the scribe? Where is the debater of this age? Has not God made foolish the wisdom of the world? For since, in the wisdom of God, the world did not know God through wisdom, God decided, through the foolishness of our proclamation, to save those who believe. For Jews*

demand signs and Greeks desire wisdom, but we proclaim Christ crucified, a stumbling block to Jews and foolishness to Gentiles, but to those who are called, both Jews and Greeks, Christ the power of God and the wisdom of God. For God's foolishness is wiser than human wisdom, and God's weakness is stronger than human strength. Consider your own call, brothers and sisters: not many were wise by human standards, not many were powerful, not many were of noble birth. But God chose what is foolish in the world to shame the wise; God chose what is weak in the world to shame the strong; God chose what is low and despised in the world, things that are not, to reduce to nothing things that are, so that no one might boast in the presence of God. He is the source of your life in Christ Jesus, who became for us wisdom from God, and righteousness and sanctification and redemption, in order that, as it is written, 'Let the one who boasts, boast in the Lord.'" [12]

From the service of "Holy Baptism":

"_____, child of God, you have been sealed by the Holy Spirit, and marked with the cross of Christ forever. Amen." [13]

"Signed, sealed, and delivered. . ." We use these words to describe something that has been completed. The contract is signed. The deal is made. The treaty is in place. Everything is as everyone wanted it. So, there is no need to worry about it. Yes, it is taken care of.

That is the way it is in baptism. Marked by the sign of the cross, we are now in the Kingdom, the heavenly Kingdom of God. Yes, God has done it all. God has given us the Holy Spirit, the Spirit who is the guarantee that enough has been done in this action by God to make us children of the Kingdom. And, yes, it is the cross of Christ that makes it possible.

Of course, *WE* might demand **MORE**. *WE* might demand some visible sign that a particular person *really* is one of God's children. We might lay down some conditions about membership in the Kingdom like a certain behavior, or a demonstration of certain gifts of the Spirit, or keeping the Ten Commandments, or living the Golden Rule, or tithing, or worship attendance, and well. . ., the list is endless.

Paul is well aware of our desire for **MORE**. He speaks of ". . . Jews demanding signs and Greeks seeking wisdom. . ." in his letter to the Corinthian congregation where there were growing factions who were demanding that members follow a certain person or do certain required things to belong. As a result, the unity of the church was being destroyed. Does that sound familiar? Yes, we have a tendency to do the very same thing. It is also true that such "human" requirements have more to do with what *WE* think *WE* can do to contribute to our salvation than they do with what God has already done!

Well, as much as you or I do not want to hear it, the Word of God says that we have NOTHING to do with our own salvation, absolutely NOTHING! Yes, that sounds foolish to us. After all, we are held accountable for our SIN and our sins; so accountable, in fact, that it cost God the life of Jesus, the Son of God. So terrible are our sins that the cross was a necessary evil to accomplish what we could not accomplish on our own, namely, our own salvation.

Certainly, Paul is right when he points out that the cross is foolishness to those who don't believe. If God were to save us, there is certainly a better way, a more convincing way, a much safer and more sanitary way to save folks. There must be another way that is **MORE** acceptable to us, and far less gory than the cross.

". . .Jews demanding signs, and Greeks seeking wisdom. . ." We are still at it! We want to depend upon ourselves, upon our wisdom, upon our smarts, upon our ingenuity, upon our power, upon our own righteousness. But the cross will not let us do that!

Nor will our baptism into Christ's death and resurrection allow us to boast at all in what *WE* have done. Signed by the cross and sealed by the Holy Spirit we must simply let that be in God's hands,

15

and under God's power. When we let it be we allow God to be God, and we finally become what we are meant to really be, namely, God's children- Christ-ians, bearers of the cross. Our concern is no longer HOW MUCH is ENOUGH to please God so that we might be saved; our concern for living is now WHAT can we do to GLORIFY GOD and love our neighbor.

Our baptism reminds us that we are NOT the source of our own life. But, as Paul says, *"(God) is the source of your life in Christ Jesus, whom God made our wisdom, our righteousness and sanctification and redemption. . ."* The sign of that presence, and that source of life in us, is the sign of the cross forever etched on our brows in the waters of baptism.

It is wisdom for us because God has removed from us our frantic seeking of something **MORE** in order to become **MORE** Christian— the implication being that the **MORE** Christian I am, the better chance I have of God accepting me. God's wisdom says, ". . .WHILE we were YET STILL sinners, Christ died for the UNgodly"![14]

The cross is righteousness for us because GOD has MADE us holy. God has removed, NO — battered down the barrier of sin with Christ's cross! God has made us righteous in Jesus. There can be NO talk of, NOR seeking of, SELF-righteousness. Our holiness is God-given. It is pure gift!

The cross is sanctification for us because it removes our need to prove *WE* are GOOD, CHRISTIAN people to God, or to each other for the purpose of being accepted, or saved. The cross is God's gift at work in us that leads us to faith and holiness. It is NOT OUR doing! We are simply to "walk in the Spirit", live under the cross, walk wet in the waters of our baptism as a simple response to God's love for us in Jesus Christ.

The cross is our redemption because God is the Person who restores and reconciles us to Himself and each other. The price for that redemption is great- the life of Jesus! So we are to live as if Christ's cross was and is of value to and for us.

This "wisdom" of God to remove any self-glory helps us to recognize God's great love for us. Because God marks us with the cross, signs us in our baptism with this cross, we KNOW that we have life, not only NOW, but forever with God in Christ! Such foolishness is the power of God at work in our lives! Indeed, we who believe God's Word of truth are fools- but fools for Christ!

Our worldly "wisdom" is thwarted! Our self-righteous seeking is ended. Something NEW has happened in our baptism. We, who are signed with the cross, and sealed by the Holy Spirit, are delivered into a new existence of grace!

Yes, we have been "signed". WE ARE GOD'S! Let us, then, boast of the Lord's great love for us by the way in which we live each day. For we have been baptized *"In the name of the Father, and of the Son, and of the Holy Spirit. Amen"!*

WEEK TWO

Baptized: Marked for Living!

CLAIMED.

THE SYMBOL OF THE DOVE

All four of the gospels (Matthew, Mark, Luke, and John) record a version of the story of Jesus' baptism by John in the Jordan River. As Jesus comes up out of the water we are told that the ". . .Spirit of God descend(s) like a dove. . ."[15]

It is also true that many, many paraments and stoles of our church bear the symbol of the dove upon them. We most often find the dove on Pentecost paraments, stoles, and banners where the dove represents the Holy Spirit. Often we also find the dove on banners, etc., that are used during baptismal and confirmation celebrations in our worship services. The dove is clearly a symbol of the Holy Spirit. In fact, "the dove is perhaps the most universal symbol used to represent the Spirit, the third member of the Trinity."[16] So, it is appropriate that we use the dove as a symbol of the Holy Spirit who has **CLAIMED** us for God's Kingdom.

THE MEDITATION

Peter writes:

> *"But you are a chosen race, a royal priesthood, a holy nation, God's own people, in order that you may proclaim the mighty acts of him who called you out of darkness into his marvelous light. Once you were not a people, but now you are God's people; once you had not received mercy, but now you have received mercy."*[17]

Reading from the service for "Holy Baptism":

"In Holy Baptism our gracious heavenly Father liberates us from sin and death by joining us to the death and resurrection of our Lord Jesus Christ. We are born children of a fallen humanity; in the waters of Baptism we are reborn children of God and inheritors of eternal life."[18]

". . . once you were not a people, but NOW YOU ARE GOD'S PEOPLE." That is how Peter describes what happens to us in baptism. We who were nothing are now something. This change has nothing to do with our ability to believe, or how good we are, or how much we know. Peter says it has to do with God's grace. ". . . once you had not received mercy, but now you have received mercy." So simple, yet so profound! God claims us as God's own because God chooses to show mercy! It is this grace, this mercy, this love that makes us who we are in Christ.

Of course, as always, our inclination is to try to take at least a little credit for what happens. We think we are somehow special. We believe that we are maybe better than someone else. We boast, at least a little, in our own goodness. We seek to claim God for ourselves. "I have decided to follow Jesus", we sing. "I know Jesus as MY personal Savior," we chirp. The words trip over our tongues, glibly proclaiming *OUR* contribution to becoming God's people.

But, that is not what the Scriptures say to us. God's WORD clearly states that the reason we belong in God's Kingdom is God's work ONLY, not ours. Because we are ". . . born children of a fallen humanity . . ." we, like Adam and Eve, sin. If left to choose on our own, we will choose our old, comfortable, sinful ways. We will NOT choose God. No matter how we try, we cannot muster up enough desire, or will power, or enough faith to choose God. We just don't have it in us. So, we need someone to come in from the outside and make us new, reclaim us from our old, sinful ways, and restore us to a right relationship.

Our righteousness in God is then, as Luther called it, "an alien righteousness". It is not something *WE* have within *US*. Instead, God comes from the outside, and chooses us. God comes to CLAIM

20

us! "*. . . once you were not a people, but now you are God's people. . .*", Peter proclaims. We are God's people because God is merciful. God chose to come among us in Jesus. God chose to be a part of our fallen humanity in order to reclaim us. God, in Jesus, chose to take on our sin, and die with it on the cross. Such is God's great love for ALL of US!

"*. . . in the waters of baptism we are reborn children of God. . .*" Yes, it is true! God is able to RE-claim us with the washing of water and the Holy Spirit in Holy Baptism. To emphasize GOD'S work and power, we baptize little children. Babes in arms are claimed for the Kingdom. They have nothing to say, nothing to bring, nothing to contribute to belonging in the Kingdom of God. This is God's great work. God chooses us BEFORE we even know what is happening. "*. . . once you were NOT a people, but NOW you are God's people.*"

Yes, this is pure gift! The GRACE of God is so vast that God has room in the Kingdom for ALL people whom God chooses. In physical birth God bestows upon each one of us the gift of earthly life. In the spiritual rebirth of baptism God claims us for an eternal life.

Once we have been claimed for God's Kingdom, we do not have to prove our value to God. For it is God who gives us value and worth, and bestows real meaning on our lives. So, we are set free to live within God's grace. We are privileged to live within God's mercy. We are blessed by God's forgiveness. CLAIMED by God, we are marked for a lifetime of service in God's Kingdom.

Yes, our true existence begins in baptism. Our life with God truly begins with the water and the Holy Spirit who CLAIMS us for God's kingdom of love and service. We are called to simply live WITHIN this gracious existence. We have been CLAIMED. Do you remember Luther's Small Catechism, Third Article, Apostles' Creed, the explanation? Luther writes: "*I believe that I CANNOT by my own understanding or effort believe in Jesus Christ my Lord, or come to him. But the Holy Spirit has called me through the Gospel. . .*" [19] Now then, let us live as if we believe that we have been called by a loving and merciful God.

". . . *once you were NOT a people, but now you are God's people. . .*" So, "*YOU ARE a chosen race, a royal priesthood, a holy nation, God's own people.*" Yes, indeed, that is who we are! God's Spirit has claimed us. We are God's children!

Amen.

WEEK THREE

Baptized: Marked for Living!

NAMED.

THE SYMBOL OF THE SIGNBOARD

The gospel writers tell us that the people who crucified Jesus were concerned about his name. They were so concerned, in fact, that they placed a signboard above his head on the cross that identified who Jesus was. Of course, some disagreed with the name the signboard gave to Jesus. So, Matthew tells it very simply: *"Over his head they put the charge against him, 'This is Jesus, the King of the Jews.'"*[20] Rather than simply naming who Jesus was, Jesus is "charged" with taking God's name for Himself- the charge of blasphemy.

In our secular world we often use name tags to identify ourselves in a gathering of people. Our name does identify us. We are unique persons. Our name also connects us to others, like our surname that connects us to a certain family. It is appropriate, then, that we use the "signboard" as the symbol for being *NAMED*.

THE MEDITATION

From the Gospel of Mark:

> *"In those days Jesus came from Nazareth of Galilee and was baptized by John in the Jordan. And just as he was coming up out of the water, he saw the heavens torn apart and the Spirit descending like a dove on him. And a voice came from heaven, 'You are my Son, the Beloved; with you I am well pleased.'"*[21]

From the service for "Holy Baptism":

"___(Name)___, I baptize you in the name of the Father, and of the Son, and of the Holy Spirit. Amen."[22]

It all begins here. Just as it began for Jesus with baptism by John in the River Jordan, so it begins for us when we are NAMED as God's children. These are such simple words, but they are no less powerful. These are the words by which Jesus commissions the disciples in the Gospel of Matthew, sending them forth into all the world to baptize, ". . . teaching them to observe all that I have commanded you . . ."[23]

Yes, it begins at the font. As the water is splashed over us, we are NAMED. "John Douglas, I baptize you in the name of . . ." The trinitarian formula is like legal statement. God legally adopts us as God's own. God calls us beloved children. An excellent way to describe what happens in baptism is to liken this act of God to the power a judge has in the adoption proceedings.

Let's say I want to adopt a child. As soon as the judge signs the papers, the child bears my name. It doesn't matter whether that child wants to have my name or not, the legal action of the judge makes that child mine. Hopefully, one day, this newly adopted child will acknowledge the reality of being my child, and want to gladly bear the family name.

So it is with baptism. God LEGALLY adopts us as children. From that point on we bear God's NAME, whether we are fully aware of it, or want to, or not! God still acts to NAME us his own.

The model of that action of God is seen in Jesus' baptism by John. Mark is concerned to share with us ". . . the gospel of Jesus Christ. . . " as he says in the first verse of his story about Jesus. It is interesting that he states that this is ". . . *the beginning of the gospel of Jesus Christ. . .*"[24] and marks that beginning with the story of Jesus' baptism by John the Baptizer. In clear and simple words Mark tells us that Jesus came to John to be baptized. *"And when He came up out of the water, immediately He saw the heavens opened and the Spirit descending upon Him like a dove; and a voice came from heaven, 'You are my Son, the Beloved; with you I am well pleased.'"*

24

Then that same Spirit drives Jesus into the wilderness to be tested before he begins his public ministry. Now NAMED "Beloved Son", Jesus is able to resist the temptations of the devil, and then begins his work as God's servant.

Yes, it seems simple enough. The simplicity of Mark's story hides the depth of God's action in all this. Though written in simple, straightforward words the impact of this brief narrative is life-changing. Jesus is the "beloved Son". He is the ONE from the house and lineage of David who is MESSIAH. The phrase, *"This is my beloved Son. . .",* is taken from Psalm 2- an enthronement psalm used ONLY when a king of the house of David was crowned king of Israel. So, Jesus IS the long-awaited Messiah from the house of David.

But, there is even more! *". . . with you I am well pleased. . ."* are words from the prophet, Isaiah, chapter 42. The context of these words is that of a suffering servant song. This suffering servant song depicts the Messiah as a SERVANT. This servant is chosen by God to suffer for all the people. Thus, put together, these two simple phrases tell us something very important about Jesus, and, ultimately, about ourselves.

God announces, as God NAMES Jesus, that this One IS the Messiah, the SERVANT-KING of David who will reveal God's plan of salvation, and even BECOME God's salvation for God's people. The public ministry of Jesus is, then, a ministry of servanthood. Jesus is to give Himself over TOTALLY to this ministry in the name of God. Jesus' ministry of complete service for others begins in Jesus' baptism. NAMED as God's "beloved", Jesus is anointed with the Spirit for service.

*"I baptize you in the **NAME** of the Father, and of the Son, and of the Holy Spirit. Amen."* As we are baptized in the NAME of the Triune God, we, too, are anointed with God's Spirit. We no longer bear our own name, we bear the name of God's "beloved sons and daughters" with whom God is well pleased. NAMED as God's, we carry that name into daily life, ministering in that name, bearing witness to that name, totally dedicated to God's work of love and grace in God's Kingdom.

Our ministry, as was Jesus', is not self-centered. It is other-focused. This is a DAILY ministry, carried out in ALL that we say and do and think. NAMED in our baptism as God's children, as Christian, we live each day AS IF this name has changed us. For we have been moved from an earthly family into a heavenly family. We have been reborn into God's family.

Through water and the Holy Spirit, our baptism into Christ's life, death, and resurrection has made us "beloved sons and daughters". Baptized into Christ's NAME, we are empowered to resist the evil schemes of the devil; and, further, we are empowered to serve in the NAME of Christ in our daily existence.

"I baptize you in the NAME of the Father, and of the Son, and of the Holy Spirit." Yes, amen! We belong to God! Let us, who are NAMED "Christ-ian" hallow that NAME among us. Let us praise God for our salvation, **AND** for our call into ministry. Let us do it by loving one another. Let us do it by living each day as servants of the Kingdom, as persons who has been NAMED as God's "beloved" children!

Amen.

WEEK FOUR

Baptized: Marked for Living!

CLOTHED.

THE SYMBOL OF THE ROBE

The symbol of the robe, or a white garment, goes back the practice of the early church when the person baptized was clothed in a white robe to signify the putting on of Christ. "The new robe signified the new person."[25] Luther also understood the symbolism of the baptismal garment. He writes at the end of his explanation of baptism in The Large Catechism:

> "Therefore let everybody regard his Baptism as the daily garment which he is to wear all the time. Every day he should be found in faith and amid its fruits, every day he should be suppressing the old man and growing up in the new."[26]

The symbolism is further enhanced by using the robe on the day of "Affirmation of Baptism". The white robe reminds those affirming their faith that they are covered in Christ. They are to continue putting on Christ until the day they die. The final use of the symbol is to use a pall to cover the casket at a person's funeral. Again, the symbol reminds us that we are covered in Christ from the beginning of our earthly walk with Christ until the last day we live on earth.

Of course, once we enter into God's heavenly Kingdom we are numbered among the white-robed saints who surround the throne of God. We have been ***CLOTHED*** for the marriage feast of the Lamb!

THE MEDITATION

Paul writes to the Colossian Christians:

27

"As God's chosen ones, holy and beloved, clothe yourselves with compassion, kindness, humility, meekness, and patience. Bear with one another and, if anyone has a complaint against another, forgive each other; just as the Lord has forgiven you, so you must also forgive. Above all, clothe yourselves with love, which binds everything together in perfect harmony. And let the peace of Christ rule in your hearts, to which indeed you were called in the one body. And be thankful. Let the word of Christ dwell in you richly; teach and admonish one another in all wisdom; and with gratitude in your hearts sing psalms, hymns, and spiritual songs to God. And whatever you do, in word or deed, do everything in the name of the Lord Jesus, giving thanks to God the Father through him."[27]

From the service of "Holy Baptism":

"Put on this robe, for in Baptism you have been clothed in the righteousness of Christ, who calls you to his great feast."[28]

Most of us have some old, favorite clothes we like to wear for bumming around the house, or doing odd jobs. Whether it's an old, worn-out pair of jeans, or an old, holey, plaid shirt, or a pair of beat-up old shoes, we put them on with joy because they are *soooo* comfortable. We feel so "at home" in them. They fit our body well because we have worn them for so long. The stiffness is long gone. We have such freedom of movement when we wear those old clothes.

Such is life in old Adam and Eve as well. We who are born in the flesh are born into a sinful condition that has been passed on for countless generations to those of us who are children of Adam and Eve. Yes, this life is so comfortable. It fits us so well, and allows for such freedom of movement! We hate to give it up. We do not want to lose control of our lives, sinful though they may be.

28

Rather, we cling to our old way of sin just the way we hang on to those old, comfortable clothes that we know so, so well. To change old ways means giving up what we know. It means taking a risk by trying something new. It means leaving behind old, well-known habits. It means giving up that which is so familiar.

That is hard for us to do on our own, in fact, impossible. So, God does it for us in baptism. God not only claims us, and signs us, and names us; God also RE-clothes us in righteousness. God gives us a new wardrobe to wear! As Paul puts is in Galatians 3: *"For as many of you as were baptized into Christ have put on Christ."*[29] That's clothing-talk. God has created us in Christ with his righteousness. It is not ours. It is God's! Baptized into Christ we have "put on" Christ. We have become his new people. Yes, we are given a new robe to wear. It is white as a sign of our purity before God. It covers our old clothes because our sin has been covered in Jesus.

Certainly, the old Adam and Eve in us does not give up easily, without a fight. Our sin seeks to retain control. We do not readily give up old, comfortable ways just as we do not readily throw away our old, holey shirt, worn-out pair of jeans, and well-worn shoes. Sin is, after all, habit-forming. It is not easily shed. That is why God has done something in Christ to us and for us. God has put Christ's cross through our sin, and covered us in Jesus' goodness. That takes place, first of all, in baptism.

"For as many of you as were baptized into Christ have put on Christ..." What does it mean... "to put on"? Does it mean to "put on airs", to be self-righteous about who we are? Does it mean we can somehow "pull ourselves up" to an acceptable level and merit God's love and mercy?

Well, of course not! As well we know, we do NOT have the power to resist sin on our own. We cannot shed the old clothing of Adam and Eve, no more than we can save ourselves from the wages of that sin's death. We NEED and HAVE someOne who has done that work for us. That One is Jesus Christ! So, in baptism we receive, as a gift, this One person's righteousness. Thus, God can look upon us as "white-robed saints" who are covered in the blood of Jesus.

But there is even more! Our new existence does not end at the font; it BEGINS there. From the moment of our baptism on, we are called to live in the righteousness bestowed upon us in Christ. This means we wear the new clothing daily so that it becomes the clothing we prefer to wear, day-in and day-out.

Paul's letter to the Colossians spells out what it means to wear this new clothing. It means compassion, kindness, lowliness, meekness, and patience. It moves us to forgive each other the wrongs we have done to each other. To wear this new clothing, above all, means to love with Christ's love. That love moves us to seek harmony and peace. This new existence causes us to be thankful as we see how much God really does love us, in spite of our sin and sins. Wearers of this new clothing seek to hear the Word of God, participate in worship as a privilege, share in the body and blood, and sing praises to GOD for his goodness!

Of course, we are imperfect now. So, our new clothing will get stained and dirty by our daily sinfulness. But, God in wisdom and mercy, washes us every day in Jesus' blood. God provides forgiveness when we fall and get dirty, or when we try to put on our old clothes again. God covers us again and again in Christ's righteousness. Our baptism into Christ never fades, nor does it fail us. Once baptized, we are clothed in Christ Jesus forever. So clothed, we are invited to live in this new clothing God has given us.

If we fall along the way and dirty ourselves, God is ready and able to pick us up, brush us off, and send us on the right way once again. If we tear a hole in the knee, God patches it with everlasting love. If we dull the whiteness of our new robe with our insistent, sinful ways, God bleaches us clean with the unfading brightener of Jesus, the Son, our Savior, the Christ. So, you who have "put on Christ" in baptism, put on the new clothing of Jesus, and live daily in these "duds of righteousness".

Amen.

WEEK FIVE

Baptized: Marked for Living!

ENLIGHTENED.

THE SYMBOL OF THE CANDLE

The candle is a very simple symbol of the light of Christ that has come into the world. The writer of John tells us early on that *". . .in the beginning was the Word. . .in him was life, and the life was the light of all people."*[30]   Jesus later, in the same gospel, proclaims himself to be *". . .the light of the world".*[31]   Thus, the lighted candle can be an appropriate symbol of the light of Christ in the baptismal service.

The symbolism of the candle given at baptism is connected to the Paschal Candle, thus reflecting the early church's practice of baptism at the Easter Vigil.[32] The candle lit from the Paschal Candle symbolizes the new light and new life that is now a part of the life of the one baptized. God's children, through the marvelous gift of Holy Baptism, have been ***ENLIGHTENED*** by the Holy Spirit. By water and the Word, the Holy Spirit calls us into faith and enlightens us with all the gifts necessary for living our new existence.

THE MEDITATION

Paul writes to the Corinthians:

> *"Therefore, since it is by God's mercy that we are engaged in this ministry, we do not lose heart. We have renounced the shameful things that one hides; we refuse to practice cunning or to falsify God's word; but by the open statement of the truth we commend ourselves to the conscience of everyone in the sight of God. And even if our gospel is veiled, it is veiled to those who are perishing. In their case*

31

the god of this world has blinded the minds of the
unbelievers, to keep them from seeing the light of
the gospel of the glory of Christ, who is the image of
God. For it is God who said, 'Let light shine out of
darkness,' who has shone in our hearts to give the
light of the knowledge of the glory of God in the face
of Jesus Christ."[33]

From the service of "Holy Baptism":

"Let your light so shine before others that they may
see your good works and glorify your Father in
heaven."[34]

Paul says to the Corinthians, *"For it is the God who said, 'Let*
light shine out of darkness', who has shone in our hearts to give
the light of the knowledge of the glory of God in the face of Christ."
The gift of light from God in baptism is the gift of Christ's Spirit at
work within us. We are enlightened. It is this gift of God that
pushes back the dark tentacles of sin, that brings light into the dark
shadows of our lives, that brightens the darkness of our sight and
heals our blindness. This light is to show forth in the way in which
we live each day as God's baptized children. Yes, we proclaim
Christ's love as the bright beacon of hope for a world filled with
darkness.

That darkness exists cannot be doubted. It's gloom fills our
hearts with fear. It's gray clouds obscure our hope. It's icy tentacles
squeeze life out of us at every possible turn. Yes, the world's
darkness is all around us. But one of the hard realities of our
existence is to realize that we, in our sin, are a part of that darkness.
Paul tells the Ephesian Christians: *". . .for once you were*
darkness. . ."[35] He doesn't say, "You were like darkness"; he says,
"you **WERE** darkness. . ."!

Because of our sin, then, we **are** darkness. So, we prefer the
darkness to the light. Like the old clothes that we prefer because
of how comfortable we are in them, so, too, though we know the
LIGHT, we still continue to walk in the darkness where we think

our sin will not be discovered. We continue to walk in the darkness where we can make all kinds of excuses as to why we **are** the way we **are**. We continue to walk in the darkness because we think nothing will be expected of us. Yes, we choose to live in the darkness rather than the light.

We **are** darkness when we ignore God's Word, the preaching and the teaching of it. We **are** darkness when we remove ourselves from the light of Christ. We **are** darkness when we become apathetic and insensitive to those around us who have needs. We **are** darkness when we seek to exclude people from this fellowship of saints and sinners because "they aren't good enough". We **are** darkness when we hinder the light of Christ from shining forth in any way in our lives.

We who **are** darkness, then, are on Satan's side, not God's. It's either/or, not both/and. We are one or the other. We are darkness and in Satan's camp, or we are light and in God's camp.

No, we don't have to be darkness. Paul says, ". . . but now you are light in the Lord."[36] Or, further, ". . . God. . . has shone in our hearts. . ." In baptism we receive the light of Christ as we are claimed as God's children. We have been forgiven! No, we do not have to continue to live in the darkness. We can, with God's mighty help, walk in the light, and **BE** light!

You know, because of the extent of the darkness in our world, it doesn't take much light to begin to push back that darkness. Think of times when you have been in a dark place, and how just a sliver of light can slice through that darkness so that you can see and make your way. Or, maybe while out walking on a dark night, you can see for miles the little light that marks your destination. One thing that strikes me as I drive through the countryside at night is how the farm lights dot the landscape for as far as you can see. These lights break through the darkness like beacons guiding my way home.

So, just a little light can go a long way. A little kindness can mend a broken heart. A little time to listen can make a person's day. A little time given to care can bring hope to an otherwise hopeless situation. A little deed of goodness can bring a smile to an otherwise sad face. A little hug, a little kiss, a smile, a little word of encouragement; all these can make a significant difference in the life of another person. Jesus talked about a little water, a little food, a shared coat. Just a little goes a long way in helping the light of Christ to shine forth in a world filled with darkness, evil, sin, and death.

"Let your light so shine before others that they may see your good works and GLORIFY your FATHER in heaven." Paul says it this way, *"For what we preach is not ourselves, but Jesus Christ as Lord, with ourselves as SERVANTS for Jesus' sake."*[37] Our good works are important as a reflection of God's love as we have experienced it in Jesus Christ our Lord. All the GLORY goes to GOD! We are not in this light-spreading business for ourselves; we are in it for Jesus' sake. We are in it to let the light of CHRIST shine through us into the world. Just as a light bulb is an instrument by which WE can see in the darkness; so, we are the servant-instruments through which others can see the LOVE of GOD. For Christ is our light and our salvation. And Christ is the light and salvation of the whole world.

Baptized into Christ, let your light so shine. . . that GOD may be GLORIFIED. Be the light you already are in Christ. Be that beacon of hope. Be that ray of love. Be that beam of kindness. For you ARE LIGHT as Christ's Spirit shines through you!

Amen.

WEEK SIX

Baptized: Marked for Living!

APPOINTED.

THE SYMBOL OF THE STOLE

The tradition of the Church reserves the wearing of the stole for clergy as an indication of their office.[38] The color of the stole reflects the seasons of the church year as do the paraments on the altar and pulpit.

However, the office of the ministry (clergy) is, in Lutheranism, only one shape of the work of ministry. By virtue of baptism, all Christians are called into a ministry of the priesthood of all believers. George Forell summarizes Martin Luther's view with these words:

> "To be a baptized Christian means to be a priest and
> the daily life of the Christian is a priestly calling in
> the world."[39]

Though there is no intention to diminish the office of the ministry, for the purposes of our reflection upon baptism, it is appropriate to use the stole as a symbol of our being ***APPOINTED*** by God for our ministry as ambassadors of God's love. One important ministry task is that of Christian parents who bring a child to be baptized and then help that child grow in faith.

THE MEDITATION

John writes:

> *"This is my commandment, that you love one another*
> *as I have loved you. No one has greater love than*
> *this, to lay down one's life for one's friends. You are*
> *my friends if you do what I command you. I do not*
> *call you servants any longer, because the servant*

does not know what the master is doing; but I have called you friends, because I have made known to you everything that I have heard from my Father. You did not choose me but I chose you. And I appointed you to go and bear fruit, fruit that will last, so that the Father will give you whatever you ask in my name. I am giving you these commands so that you may love one another."[40]

From the service of "Holy Baptism":

"In Christian love you have presented this child for Holy Baptism. You should, therefore, faithfully bring him to the services of God's house, and teach her the Lord's Prayer, the Creed, and the Ten Commandments. As he grows in years, you should place in her hands the Holy Scriptures and provide for his instruction in the Christian faith, that, living in the covenant of her Baptism and in communion with the Church, he may lead a Godly life until the day of Jesus Christ."
"Do you promise to fulfill these obligations?"[41]

Jesus says, "You did not choose me, but I chose you and appointed you that you should go and bear fruit. . ." These words of Jesus are in the context of the great commandment to ". . . love one another as I have loved you." I would suggest that one of the greatest acts of love by a parent is to bring a child for Holy Baptism. It is an act of love because at the font we give our child over into God's gracious hands. We, in effect, give up our primary claim on our child, and turn this young life over to God. To bring a child to receive this gift of new life from our gracious God is, indeed, a great act of love.

Yet, it is even more than that. God has ". . . appointed us to bear fruit. . ." As parents we are appointed as guardians of GOD'S CHILDREN. As guardians, we are given the task of "standing in" for God in raising God's little ones in a Christian environment.

36

So, we make a promise at the baptism of our children. We promise, in essence, to do everything we can to help this child realize that he/she is God's chosen child. We are appointed to bring, teach, place, and provide. To what end? So that our children might live in the covenant God has made with them, and lead Godly lives in communion with others.

No, we don't bring our children for baptism in order to fulfill our appointed "duty" as a parent in relationship to the church. We don't do it because it is the "right" thing to do. We do this so that our children might be given over to God in Jesus Christ. We do it so that we might be reminded of our responsibility for God's children in helping them to grow in faith and love towards God and others. Charlie Shedd, in his book, <u>You Can Be a Great Parent</u>, says that the greatest, single thing a parent can do for a child is ". . . to put your hand in the hand of your Heavenly Father."[42]

Yes, this is an awesome responsibility. Oh, there are times when we fail miserably. We will make many mistakes with God's children. But that does not disqualify us from the task of guardianship. As stewards of God's grace and God's children, we aid the faith-growth of God's people. Having brought a child to the font, we are appointed to the task of Christian parenting. We are given the opportunity to love in a special way. We are chosen to "be Christ" for and to God's children so that they may know Christ as Lord and Savior.

That raises a very sticky issue among us. What does this awesome responsibility entail? Every study that I know of, those that study the effects of the parents' faith-life upon their children, indicate some startling numbers. There is a direct correlation between the faith-life of parents and the faith-life of their children. If parents are active in regular worship and demonstrate that the Christian faith is important in their daily lives, there is a very good chance that their children will do the same. If, on the other hand, parents show no interest in the church, their children will likely be as apathetic.

What does it mean to demonstrate faith? Our children learn more by what they see than by what they hear. If we drop off our children and then pick them up from Sunday School *(Sunday School is important for children, you know!)* without including worship as an important part of our lives; what have we taught our kids? What kinds of excuses do our children hear from us about not going to worship? What are we teaching them? How important is it that our kids know the content of the Christian faith so that it has some meaning and impact on their daily lives?

Parents, grandparents, sponsors- there are plenty of people like David Koresh in the world who would gladly swoop up your kids and lead them away into some, far-out, even evil cults. The less we live our faith, the greater chance such groups can attract our kids. God appoints us to bear fruit- in this case, to help our kids know Jesus as Lord.

What do we do if, when after parents have brought their children for baptism, they disappear from worship? They do not bring, nor teach, nor place, nor provide for these newborns in Christ. They do not seem to take their guardianship of God's children very seriously. They let their appointment as God's stewards slip away. What do we do? Do we point fingers at them, condemning them for their laxity? No, I suspect such action might drive them even further away from the church. So, what then?

I would suggest that we pray for each family that brings a child to God in baptism. As we pray, we might discover that God can use us to help those parents raise these reborn little ones in a Christian environment. We, who witness the baptisms of God's children, do have a responsibility. We, too, are appointed as caretakers, as guardians, as ambassadors to these children of God's love in Christ for them. God has chosen us and appointed us to the ministry of love of others, including these little children who are signed, claimed, named, clothed, and enlightened in baptism.

It seems, then, that we, as a community of faith into which a child has been grafted through water and the Spirit, have some rights. If parents neglect their calling as guardians, we are called and appointed to step in and carry out that calling as guardians. When a child has the opportunity to be in Sunday School at age three and older, we, as God's people, can ask those parents bring God's child to Sunday School and worship as part of their appointment as guardians. If they refuse, we might offer to do it in their place. That may seem radical! But, if we are to take our appointment seriously, can we sit back and let God's children disappear from our Lord's presence, from the life-giving presence of Word and Sacrament?

All I'm saying is that we need to see baptism, not as some kind of magical formula that protects our children forever no matter what we or they do; rather we need to understand that baptism is a living covenant, a living will and testament, if you please, that calls us to bring, teach, place, and provide for God's children in every way as we have opportunity, so that they might continue to live and grow in this gracious covenant all the days of their lives. As we take seriously the "daily-ness" of baptism, we will begin to understand what it means to love each other in Christ. We will also understand that we are no longer servants, but "friends" of Christ, who do His bidding joyfully.

"Do you promise to fulfill these obligations?"

As guardians of God's children, may we joyfully say, "Yes!"

Amen.

MAUNDY THURSDAY

Baptized: Marked for Living!

WASHED.

THE SYMBOL OF THE SHELL

Jesus tells Nicodemus that he must *". . . be born again of water and the Spirit. . ."* in order to enter the Kingdom of heaven.[43] It is clear from this word of Jesus that water is very important as the element used to convey God's grace in the new birth in baptism by the Holy Spirit. Baptism is a washing. In this washing of baptism, the pastor may choose to use a shell for pouring the water, ". . .to insure the use of a generous quantity of water."[44]

Also, in early Jewish and Christian art, the shell became a symbol for immortality. In its marine connotations, the shell became a symbol for baptism. Thus, the shell and the water together point out the profound reality of baptism as a new birth of God's children who have been given the gift of eternal life.[45] As God's children, we have been *WASHED*.

THE MEDITATION

Peter writes:

> *"For Christ also suffered for sins once for all, the righteous for the unrighteous, in order to bring you to God. He was put to death in the flesh, but made alive in the Spirit, in which he went and made a proclamation to the spirits in prison, who in former times did not obey, when God waited patiently in the days of Noah, during the building of the ark, in which a few, that is eight persons, were saved through water. And baptism, which this prefigured, now saves you- not as a removal of dirt from the body, but as an appeal to God for a good conscience, through*

the resurrection of Jesus Christ, who has gone into heaven and is at the right hand of God, with angels, authorities, and powers made subject to him. "[46]

From the service of "Holy Baptism":

"Holy God, mighty Lord, gracious Father: we give you thanks, for in the beginning your Spirit moved over the waters and you created heaven and earth. By the gift of water you nourish and sustain us and all living things. By the waters of the flood you condemned the wicked and saved those whom you had chosen, Noah and his family. You led Israel by the pillar of cloud and fire through the sea, out of slavery into the freedom of the promised land. In the waters of the Jordan your Son was baptized by John and anointed with the Holy Spirit. By the baptism of His own death and resurrection your beloved Son has set us free from the bondage of sin and death, and has opened the way to the joy and freedom of everlasting life. He made water a sign of the kingdom and of cleansing and rebirth. In obedience to His command, we make disciples of all nations, baptizing them in the name of the Father, and of the Son, and of the Holy Spirit.
Pour out your Holy Spirit, so that those who are here baptized may be given new life. Wash away the sin of all those who are cleansed by this water and bring them forth as inheritors of your glorious kingdom."[47]

Washing. Making clean. Purifying. There is something wonderful about feeling clean! After the grime of the day has been washed away in a hot, soothing bath or shower, we feel new and refreshed, and squeaky clean. We slip into fresh clothing, made clean in the churning waters of the washing machine. It's so good to feel and smell and be clean. Yes, there's something nice and fresh and clean and pure about it all.

Paul makes the analogy for us: *"Baptism NOW saves you, not as removal of dirt from the body but as an appeal to God for a clear conscience, through the resurrection of Christ. . ."* Yes, our baptism is also a washing. The service calls it a ". . . wash(ing) away of sin. . . a cleansing by this water. . ."

We who are born in SIN (Adam and Eve's SIN) need a good washing, a good cleaning up. Our lives are messed up and filthy even though we come as innocent babes in the arms of loved ones to be baptized. Though, as babies, we may not have willfully sinned, we are in SIN. We participate in the age-old rebellion of Adam and Eve. For we too, left to ourselves, without any action on God's part to change us, will and do rebel against God. We will NOT choose God! We will NOT believe in Christ! Try as we may, we do not have it within us to believe. So, God does something about it. God comes in the washing of the waters of baptism. God cleans us up. God scrubs out the stain of Sin. God covers us with new clothing, the pure, life-giving clothing of Christ's righteousness.

Luther says, in his explanation of the Third Article of the Apostles' Creed: *"I CANNOT BY MY OWN understanding or effort believe in Jesus Christ my Lord nor come to Him, but the Holy Spirit calls me through the gospel, enlightens me with his gifts, and keeps me in the one true faith. . ."*[48] Yes, this washing is God's act. As the water washes over us, God's Spirit fills our lives and makes us clean and whole and pure and God's!

On this Maundy Thursday it is appropriate for us to talk of washing. For it was on Christ's last night with his disciples that Jesus expanded the meaning of washing. Jesus took a basin of water and a towel and washed the disciples' feet[49]- a sign of servanthood. We who are washed in the waters of baptism are called forth into a similar service. We who have been washed are called to live in that washing by being of loving service to those around us.

Washed, we wash. Loved, we love. Served, we serve. Our baptism is not just a past event. It is also a present reality. Made God's children through this washing of water in baptism, we wash, that is, we serve others in their need. Cleansed by this water, we seek to live as Christ's disciples in a world in desperate need of new life and cleansing.

The waters of baptism have washed over us. We have been made new. We have been cleansed. We have been refreshed. We are born again to a new and living hope given to us in Jesus Christ our Lord. Having been so washed, may we be foot-washers, people of faith who serve.

Amen.

EASTER SUNDAY

Baptized: Marked for Living!

RAISED.

THE SYMBOL OF THE LILY(FLOWER)

One of the wonderful pictures used by the scriptures for the new life given by God is written by the prophet Isaiah. In chapter 35 the prophet paints a beautiful portrait of new life as he writes:

> *"The wilderness and the dry land shall be glad,*
> *the desert shall rejoice and blossom;*
> *like the crocus it shall blossom abundantly,*
> *and rejoice with joy and singing."*[50]

The blooming of the desert is a sign of God's salvation for his people. So, it is appropriate that one of the powerful symbols of Easter is a flower, the lily. The white Easter lily is a common symbol for Easter. Often our churches are filled with the beauty and fragrance of these symbols of new life. The springing forth of such beauty from the dead bulb and the "symbolic purity of its color have come to represent the resurrection."[51]

THE MEDITATION

Matthew writes:

> *"After the sabbath, as the first day of the week was dawning, Mary Magdalene and the other Mary went to the tomb. And suddenly there was a great earthquake; for an angel of the Lord, descending from heaven, came and rolled back the stone and sat on it. His appearance was like lightning, and his clothing white as snow. For fear of him the guards shook and became like dead men. But the angel said*

45

*to the women, 'Do not be afraid; I know that you are
looking for Jesus who was crucified. He is not here;
for he has been raised as he said. Come, see the
place where he lay. Then go quickly and tell his
disciples, He has been raised from the dead, and
indeed he is going ahead of you to Galilee; there
you will see him. This is my message for you.' So
they left the tomb quickly with fear and great joy,
and ran to tell his disciples. Suddenly Jesus met them
and said, 'Greeting!' And they came to him, took
hold of his feet, and worshiped him. Then Jesus said
to them, 'Do not be afraid; go and tell my brothers
to go to Galilee; there they will see me.'"[52]*

From the service of "Holy Baptism":

"God, the Father of our Lord Jesus Christ, we give
you thanks for freeing your sons and daughters from
the power of sin and for raising them up to a new
life through this holy sacrament. Pour your Holy
Spirit upon us: the Spirit of wisdom and
understanding, the Spirit of counsel and might,the
Spirit of knowledge and the fear of the Lord, the
Spirit of joy in your presence."[53]

It is Easter. It is time, after the horrors and death of Good
Friday, to celebrate the joy of resurrection and new life. Our journey
through Lent has been a time of reflection upon both Good Friday
and Easter. Maybe by now you have made the connections between
our baptism into the death and resurrection of Jesus Christ and the
events of the last days of Jesus' life on earth, namely, Good Friday
and Easter.

We who are drowned in the waters of baptism are raised to a
new life. Not only do the waters kill us, they now nurture us with
new life. We who were born in Sin, are cleansed and set free from
that Sin. We do not HAVE to continue in our old ways; we have
been put into a new relationship, and been given a new way to live.

46

That is the genius of God's work in baptism. God killed and is killing the old Adam and Eve in us so that the new persons in Christ might live to the glory of our Lord's name!

Yes, that is what this day is all about. Easter is a celebration of new life. It is not just a rite of spring whereby we notice all of the signs of the earth's new life around us. That is good, but it is not enough to experience only the earthly forms of new life. We are called to remember, and thereby participate in, the spiritual new life we have in baptism. In so doing, we praise God. We thank the Lord for the new life we have received in Christ.

The story of the resurrection of Jesus, then, becomes our story. Paul tells it best: *"We were buried with Him by baptism into death, so that as Christ was raised from the dead by the glory of the Father, we too might walk in newness of life. For if we have been united with Him in a death like His, we shall certainly be united with Him in a resurrection like His."*[54] Notice the active verb used to describe our new existence. We are raised so that we ". . .might WALK in newness of life." No resting on our laurels here, or should I say on God's laurels (for it is God who has saved us, not we ourselves). No sitting back. No marking this date in our Bible as the date we were saved, and depending upon that to keep us safe. NO! We are to WALK in newness of life.

Yes, we are on a journey. Yes, the path is filled with dead ends, wrong turns, rocks, and potholes. This pilgrimage on earth is not an easy nor safe trip. However, our baptism into Christ reminds us that we do not travel alone. God is always with us. The God who has given us new life in baptism gives us that new life each and every day. The God who set us free from Sin, now daily gives us the power to resist that Sin. So, we WALK. We live. We go forth into the daily tasks and duties of life on earth with the certain hope that we are saved. God has seen to that by raising Jesus from the dead. Yes, we are free to walk in newness of life. We are free to live as born again people, Easter people. That is what it means to be baptized- it is daily resurrection practice. It is daily dying to sin, and daily rising to live. It is walking in the Spirit given to us in our baptism.

So, today, as you re-affirmed your baptism, remember that this is a life-long covenant that God has made with you. God will never give up on you. Though you may stray, God is ready and willing to take you back at any time. Though we may fall along the way, God is able to put us back on our feet again. Though we make wrong turns, God always forgives. So, today we say "YES" again to the God who has proclaimed His "YES!" to us in Jesus the Christ.

Alleluia! Jesus lives! And so do we!

Amen.

APPENDIX A

HOME ALTAR INSTRUCTIONS

CROSS

The cross can be made out of any material a person might choose, preferably wood of some kind. It should be about a foot high and the cross arm should be about six inches. The wood should be at least three-quarters of an inch square. The cross should have a base so that it is free-standing.

DOVE

The dove can be made out of stiff paper in any pattern a person might choose. The dove is placed at the top of the vertical arm of the cross (simply tape it in place).

SIGNBOARD

The signboard is made by cutting tag board into one-half by two inch strips. A hole is punched in the two corners of one long side. A piece of yarn is tied in each hole so that the signboard might hang on the cross. People are encouraged to put their family name on the signboard with the word "Christian" underneath their name.

ROBE

Use white, light cotton cloth (an old sheet would do) to make the robe. Cut the fabric into oblong shapes about six inches long and 3 inches wide. In the very center of the piece of cloth cut out a square hole big enough to fit over the vertical arm of the cross.

CANDLE

Use white candles no taller than four inches (We used old candles from Christmas Eve candlelighting services). Put them into plastic communion glasses, securing them in place with plaster. The candles can then stand on the base of the cross.

STOLE

Use a red cloth (any light-weight material will work). Simply cut strips about one inch wide and five to six inches long out of the material. Drape the strip of red material around the vertical arm of the cross.

SHELL

Try to find shells about the size of a quarter. They can be purchased or maybe someone can pick them up along the seashore. If real shells are used, they are placed on the base of the cross. Another option would be to cut "baptismal-shaped" shells out of white tagboard and hang them on the horizontal arm of the cross.

LILY/FLOWER

One can make a lily-shaped flower out of paper. Use a green pipecleaner as the stem. Or, look for white lily-like flowers in a craft store. Either way, use a white ribbon to tie them to the vertical arm of the cross at its base.

PUTTING IT ALL TOGETHER

When the home altar is completely assembled, the robe should be draped over the cross. The stole and signboard should be draped over the cross on top of the robe. The dove should be attached to the very top of the cross. The candle and the shell should be standing on the base. The lily/flower should be attached with a ribbon to the foot of the cross. See the photo on the next page.

Photo of "Home Altar"

APPENDIX B

SANCTUARY PREPARATIONS

If the church has a large cross in the front, use it as a visual aid to carry the theme of this series throughout the Lenten season. Make pieces similar to the home altar, only large enough to match the size of the cross in the sanctuary. If the church does not have a large cross in the chancel/nave, make a free-standing cross on which all of the symbols might be placed during the series. Using a cross in the worship center is an excellent way to keep the theme of the Lenten-Easter series before the members of the congregation.

The cover of this book is an example of how a sanctuary might be decorated.

APPENDIX C

NOTES ON USE OF
THE SERVICE OF HOLY BAPTISM

Developing a baptismal ministry of the parish is very important. The process begins as families await the birth of a child. As Christians, the new birth in baptism is as significant as the physical birth of a child. Our concern is to demonstrate how important baptismal life is for God's people. A learning experience such as this Lent-Easter series is helpful. It is also helpful to match actual baptismal practice with the learning that is, or has taken place, within a parish setting.

The following are some notes on how we might apply our learning to the actual service of Holy Baptism using the wonderful service we have in our Lutheran Book of Worship[55]. These notes are only suggestions on how to incorporate the symbolism developed in this series into the worship life of our congregations.

First of all, it is always preferable to administer the Sacrament of Holy Baptism at the regular worship service of the gathered congregation. A child is not only reborn into the new life God has created through this sacrament; a child is baptized into a new family, the congregation of God's people. It is also preferable that the baptismal font hold a central place in the nave of the church. A highly visible font is a constant reminder of how God's people have entered into God's family of faith.

As the people gather for worship, a baptismal banner could stand in the chancel area with the lighted paschal candle near it. The banner could have the child(ren)'s name on it. This same baptismal banner (and lighted paschal candle) could be present when baptized members of the congregation reaffirm their baptism (confirmation) and be present when the community gathers for the funeral service of one of its members. The use of such a banner for all of these "stages of life" is a reminder that we who are named in Christ are placed into a life-long journey of fulfilling our baptism.

Baptism is a daily experience of God's grace. It is not complete until our death in Christ.

Finally, as to the placement of the baptism within the worship service, I think it should be the first act of worship. Placing it first indicates how important this act of God is. God's first act in our lives is to adopt us as children of the Kingdom. Also, beginning with the baptism means we are going to take our time and not rush through this sacrament. Often, when baptisms are placed later in the worship service, we might feel pressed for time and make all present feel as if this is a "hurry-up job" to be taken care of as we have the time. So, to avoid that message, I would encourage the congregation to begin worship with baptism.

Notes on the rubrics:

1. While a baptismal hymn is sung, the candidates, sponsors, and parents gather at the font.

Small children might also be asked to gather at the font as part of the baptismal party. This allows them to see and hear everything that happens in this sacrament close at hand. They might even get wet when the water is poured into the font! The pastor could also, on occasion, pause to make the sign of the cross on the forehead of each child after the child(ren) have witnessed the baptism so close at hand. It is an excellent reminder of the need for remembering and living in our baptism each day.

2. The minister addresses the baptismal group and the congregation.

Hopefully, the minister does this in such a way that the congregation knows it is being addressed as well as the baptismal party. It is important that the gathered people understand their participation in this powerful work of God!

3. A sponsor for each candidate, in turn, presents the candidate with these or similar words: or *4. The minister addresses those candidates who are able to answer for themselves:*

This is very straight forward. I would encourage the sponsors, if there is more than one, to say "We" present rather than "I" present. The sponsors will present each child with their first and middle names.

5. The minister addresses the sponsors and parents.

6. When only young children are baptized, the minister says:

After the parents and sponsors respond "I do" we place a white stole around the necks of each parent as a sign that they have been yoked to the very important office of Christian parenting. Remembering that the stole is a sign of the office of the ministry, we carry that same sign into this very important office of ministry among the priesthood of all believers. To carry this symbolism one step further, every confirmand receives a red stole during the service of "Reaffirmation of Baptism" (confirmation). It is given to them prior to the actual rite so that they might "design" them with appropriate symbols. During the rite the parents place these stoles around the necks of the youth, thus "transferring" major responsibility for continued growth in the Christian faith to the person who is reaffirming their baptism.

9. The minister begins with the thanksgiving.

Just prior to the thanksgiving we pour the water into the font, letting it splash so that all present might hear and see the element used in this sacrament.

10. The minister addresses the baptismal group and the congregation.

We make the renouncing of evil and the devil into three questions. This reflects the earliest baptismal liturgies. It also emphasizes our rejection of evil. Further, it better matches the three- part confession of the Apostles' Creed.

11. The minister baptizes each candidate.

Whichever formula is used, use plenty of water. Splash it around! Get the baptismal party a little wet. Let the children standing close by feel the water and hear the water in the baptism. After we baptize the minister takes the child out into the congregation to present the child to the gathered people of God. The minister announces that this child is now God's child and a member of this family of faith. The minister encourages the gathered family to pray for and support the parents and sponsors who have brought this new child of God to be baptized. The people are also asked to help in any way so that this child might grow in the Christian faith. Upon returning to the font the minister gives the child to a parent. The service continues with the greeting in rubric 12.

14. The minister marks the sign of the cross on the forehead of each of the baptized. Oil prepared for this purpose may be used. As a sign of the cross is made, the minister says:

The importance of the mark of the cross cannot be underestimated. If oil is not used the minister may dip his/her thumb in the baptismal waters again and make the mark using water. To carry this symbolism even further, just prior to the "commendation" in the "Burial of the Dead" service, the minister might dip his/her hands into water in the font and make the sign of the cross on the casket as a reminder that the cross that marked us as God's is the same cross that now saves us in death. Our baptism is complete!
At this point the minister may place on the child a baptismal gown (bib) as a sign that this child is clothed in Christ. The symbolism of being "clothed" is also a part of the rite of "Affirmation of Baptism" when we place a white robe on those being confirmed. Further, we would suggest using a pall to cover the casket at a funeral. From the beginning of our new life with God until we die we are clothed in Christ. God sees us as new persons, washed clean in the blood of our Savior!

16. A lighted candle may be given to each of the baptized (to the sponsor of a young child) by a representative of the congregation who says:

We give the candle to a parent who goes to the paschal candle, lights the baptismal candle, then places it in a holder on the altar. Upon returning to the font, we speak the words.

18. The ministers and the baptismal group turn toward the congregation; a representative of the congregation says:

In our parish the children who have come forward to see the baptism close at hand, the minister, the baptismal party all move into the center of the nave. The congregation stands. Together we welcome this new person into the family with the words suggested. We exchange the peace. As we return to our places for worship, we sing the last verses of the baptismal hymn. Then the service continues with the "Prayer of the Day".

BIBLIOGRAPHY

Forell, George. "Baptism and the Universal Priesthood of All Believers" in Trinity Seminary Review. Vol. 6. No. 1. Spring 1984.

Keifert, Patrick. "A Public Ministry by All the Baptized?" in Word and World. Vol. VII. No. 4. Fall 1987.

Luther, Martin. Luther's Works. American Edition. Vol. 51. Gen. ed. Helmut T. Lehmann. Philadelphia: Fortress Press, 1959.

Lutheran Book of Worship. Minneapolis: Augsburg Publishing, 1978.

Moe, Dean. Christian Symbols Handbook. Minneapolis: Augsburg Publishing, 1985.

New Revised Standard Version of the Holy Bible. Grand Rapids: Zondervan, 1990.

Pederson, Phillip E. Ed. What Does This Mean?: Luther's Catechisms Today. Minneapolis: Augsburg Publishing, 1979.

Pfatteicher, Philip E. Commentary on the Lutheran Book of Worship. Minneapolis: Augsburg Publishing, 1990.

Pfatteicher, Philip E. and Carlos R. Messerli. Manual on the Liturgy: Lutheran Book of Worship. Minneapolis: Augsburg Publishing, 1979.

Shedd, Charlie. You Can Be a Great Parent. Waco: Word Books, 1970.

Tappert, Theodore G. Trans. and ed. The Book of Concord. Philadelphia: Fortress Press, 1959.

NOTES

[1]   Theodore G. Tappert, trans. and ed., The Book of Concord, (Philadelphia: Fortress Press, 1959), p. 441-442.

[2]   Phillip E. Pederson, ed., What Does This Mean?: Luther's Catechisms Today, (Minneapolis: Augsburg Publishing, 1979), p. 153.

[3]   1 Peter 3:21. Note: All scriptural references will be from the New Revised Standard Version of the Holy Bible, (Grand Rapids: Zondervan, 1990) unless otherwise noted.

[4]   Luther's Works, Vol. 51, Gen. ed., Helmut T. Lehmann, (Philadelphia: Fortress Press, 1959), p. 328.

[5]   Inter-Lutheran Commission on Worship, Lutheran Book of Worship, (Minneapolis: Augsburg Publishing, 1978), p. 121. From now on this work will be referred to as LBW.

[6]   Luke 10:25-39. The Greek word in this sentence for "justify" means "to make oneself look good".

[7]   For example, Leviticus 19 talks about various people who are considered "neighbor", including the "poor" and the "alien" listed in 19:10.

[8]   Patrick Keifert, "A Public Ministry by All the Baptized?", Word and World, Vol. VII, No. 4 (Fall 1987), p. 358.

[9]   Philip E.Pfatteicher, Commentary on the Lutheran Book of Worship, (Minneapolis: Augsburg Publishing, 1990), p. 223.

[10]   1 Corinthians 2:2.

[11]   Pfatteicher, op. cit., p. 224.

[12] 1 Corinthians 1:18-31.

[13] LBW, p. 124.

[14] Romans 5:6-8.

[15] Matthew 3:13-17.

[16] Dean Moe, Christian Symbols Handbook, (Minneapolis: Augsburg Publishing, 1985), p. 26.

[17] 1 Peter 2:9-10.

[18] LBW, p. 121.

[19] Pederson, op. cit., p. 120.

[20] Matthew 27:37.

[21] Mark 1:9-12.

[22] LBW, p. 123.

[23] Matthew 28:18-20.

[24] Mark 1:1.

[25] Pfatteicher, op. cit., p. 56-57.

[26] Tappert, op. cit., p. 446.

[27] Colossians 3:12-17.

[28] Pfatteicher, op. cit., p. 58.

[29] Galatians 3:27.

[30]   John 1:1,4.

[31]   John 8:12.

[32]   Pfatteicher, op. cit., p. 58.

[33]   2 Corinthians 4:1-6.

[34]   LBW, p. 124.

[35]   Ephesians 5:8a.

[36]   Ephesians 5:8b.

[37]   2 Corinthians 4:5.

[38]   Philip E. Pfatteicher and Carlos R. Messerli, Manual on the Liturgy:LBW, (Minneapolis: Augsburg Publishing, 1979), p. 160.

[39]   George Forell, "Baptism and the Universal Priesthood of All Believers", Trinity Seminary Review, Vol. 6, No. 1 (Spr. 1984), p. 35.

[40]   John 15:12-17.

[41]   LBW, p. 121.

[42]   Charlie Shedd, You Can Be a Great Parent, (Waco: Word Books, 1970), p. 15.

[43]   John 3:5.

[44]   Pfatteicher and Messerli, op. cit., p. 181.

[45]   Moe, op. cit., p. 52.

[46]   1 Peter 3:18-22.

47   LBW, p. 122.

48   Pederson, op. cit., p.

49   John 13:1-20.

50   Isaiah 35:1-2a.

51   Moe, op. cit., p. 23.

52   Matthew 28:1-10.

53   LBW, p. 124.

54   Romans 6:4-5.

55   All references are to "Holy Baptism", LBW, p. 121-125.